Table of Contents

Your Free Gift

As a way of saying thank you for your purchase, I'm offering a copy of my book to help you get started with hunting affordably.

In *"21 Simple Steps to Save Big Money on Hunting Equipment",* you will my learn stratigies to help you save 30% or more on hunting gear. My goal is to help people get into hunting regardless of their budget.

Visit http://bit.ly/savemoneyonhunting to Grab Your FREE Copy of "21 Simple Steps to Save Big Money on Hunting Equipment".

Pheasant Hunting Success is here in this Book.

We teach you all of the essentials to getting started with pheasant hunting. It is our goal to save you the pain, heartache and lost time that many hunters experience when they start pheasant hunting.

Attention All Struggling Pheasant Hunters

"This Is A Step-By-Step Guide To Pheasant Hunting Success With No Step Missed!"

Here are a few of the topics covered in **"Pheasant Hunting Made Simple"**:

- How to Get Started Affordably

- Best Guns for Pheasant Hunting

- How to get Permission to Hunt Private Land

- Understanding What to Do When You are in the Fields

- How to Party Hunt for Pheasants

- Shooting Techniques

- Pheasant Cleaning

- and much more…

Example of the hunting diagrams and pictures included:

How to Party Hunt for Pheasants

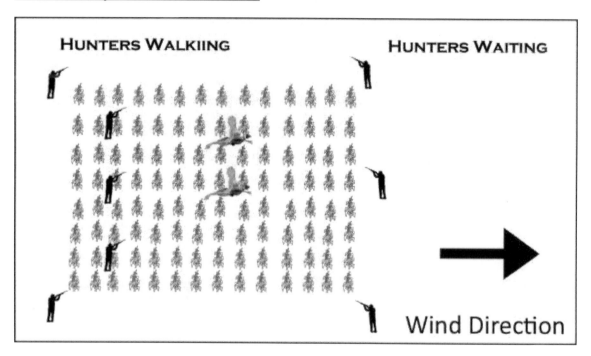

If you enjoy this book you may also enjoy my other books:

Scott's Author Page: http://bit.ly/scottsauthorpage

Attention All Struggling Pheasant Hunters...

"Finally A Comprehensive Resource For Pheasant Hunting All In One Place. Never Has It Been So Easy To Start Pheasant Hunting!"

What are the common mistakes of beginners?

1. Poor shooting techniques

2. Not understanding pheasant habits

3. Don't know how to identify pheasants

How Do You Avoid These Mistakes?

In this book we will show you easy to learn techniques that will help you immediately improve your pheasant hunting success. Put these lessons into action to avoid beginner mistakes.

Hunting for Pheasant can be one of the best ways to enjoy the outdoors. By using the techniques in this book you will be able to greatly improve your pheasant hunting success.

You will learn to avoid these many, many mistakes and understand all of the basics for pheasant hunting, allowing you to achieve pheasant hunting success fast!

What Will You Learn?

Our goal is to help you understand pheasant habits, proper preparation, shooting stratigies and more. This book will accelerate your learning to shoot more pheasants.

Overview:

- To begin, we will review the equipment you need including clothing, firearms and what to bring on your hunt, plus more…

- Next we cover where to hunt, how to get permission to hunt private land and detailed hunting instructions.

- The final portion of this book covers shooting techniques and what to do after you shoot.

Who Can Benefit from This Book?
We provide relevant information for Pheasant hunters trying to improve their success:

- Novice Pheasant hunters

- Pheasant hunters struggling for success

- People exited to start Pheasant hunting

If you have never hunted pheasants before you will get an in depth overview of all of the skills for a successful hunt.

Now let's get started…

Step 1: Clothing

Appropriate Clothing for Pheasant Hunting

The temperature during pheasant hunting seasons can vary greatly so it is important to dress properly for the time of year that you will be hunting pheasants. In most areas pheasant hunting is done in the fall and early winter so you need to have clothes that will allow you to remain warm during these cooler times.

Additionally, in most pheasant hunting situations you need to have blaze orange clothing covering the top ½ or your body. This is to make you easy for other hunters to see to ensure that people do not shoot in your direction.

Pheasant hunting seasons commonly overlap with other hunting seasons such as rabbit, squirrel, quail and even deer hunting. You absolutely want to be sure to follow the laws for your area and ensure that you wear blaze orange. Even if it is not a requirement in your area I would recommend it to increase visibility.

Here are the items that you will want to have:

- Blaze orange coat or vest over another coat

- Blaze orange baseball hat or stalking cap

- Thick jeans for the fall, snow style hunting pants in the winter

- Long johns/long underwear depending on the temperature

- Gloves

- Hunting boots

- Wool Socks, depending on temperature

Blaze Orange Coat or Blaze Orange Vest

Depending on where you live and the time of season that you are hunting for pheasants you will encounter a large range of temperatures. Temperatures for early season hunting could easily be 60-70 degrees. In contrast, temperatures in December could be below zero.

You could choose from two different ways to ensure that you have the top ½ of your body covered with blaze orange. You could either invest in a blaze orange hunting jacket or you could get a blaze orange hunting vest.

In my case, I hunt for deer as well so in the winter I can use my hunting coat that I use for deer hunting when I go pheasant hunting. However, I want to encourage you that it is not necessary to go out and buy a brand new jacket. Maybe you already have a camouflage or other warm jacket so all you have to do is purchase a hunting vest to put over your coat. Vests can be very inexpensive, typically around $20 or $30.

The other nice thing about having a hunting vest is you can use them in the warmer days over a long sleeve shirt or sweatshirt. There are many days that I hunt for pheasant where all you need is a long sleeve shirt and the vest makes it very convenient to get into legal hunting apparel.

Blaze Orange Baseball Hat or Stalking Hat

In the warmer fall days, a blaze orange baseball hat is what I use for my pheasant hunting trips. These hats ensure that I have enough orange on to be seen by fellow hunters. Additionally, the baseball hat style allows my ears to be open and uncovered allowing me to listen for pheasants without any sound lost.

When the temperatures dip as the season progresses you may want to covert over to a blaze orange stalking hat. Again, the blaze orange increases visibility to the rest of your hunting party and any other hunters that may be in the area.

Stalking hats provide plenty of warmth as the year gets colder. They might dampen a little bit of the sound as you try to listen for pheasants but I would rather have that issue over freezing my ears off. Some stalking hats convert into facemasks which could be very nice if you are hunting a very cold day.

Thick Jeans for the Fall, Warm Hunting Style Snow Pants for the Winter

Fall days that are warm call for a thick pair of jeans. Jeans allow you plenty of freedom of movement and they also provide good protection from thorns, branches, fences and other items that you may encounter when you are pheasant hunting.

Remember not to wear brand new jeans that you want to keep nice for your regular daytime activities. This is a great opportunity to pull out that old pair of jeans from your closet that still fits you but are no longer in style or you just don't like them.

I recommend this because it is very likely that at some point during one of your hunting trips you are going to get the jeans dirty or rip a hole in them from a branch or catch them on a barb wire fence.

When hunting in the later season you may need to put on some type of warm hunting snow pants on over your jeans. Again, I hunt deer as well so I already have a pair of blaze orange snow pants. If you do not have blaze orange snow pants that is ok because most regulations only call for the top ½ of your body to be covered with blaze orange.

Similar to my recommendation with jeans, you want to be aware that it is very likely to get these pants dirty or even tear them so don't wear brand new clothes that you would not want to get ruined.

Long Johns/Long Underwear Depending on Temperature

This will depend on the time of season. For those days that are very cold outside, it can add a level of comfort by wearing warm long underwear.

In addition to the time of the year, the type of hunting you plan on doing may impact your choice to wear long underwear or not. If you are doing a lot of hunting drives and you are the person standing and waiting for pheasants to come to you there is a chance that you will get colder than those people who are actively walking to scare up pheasants.

Gloves

Sometimes in the early season I elect to go pheasant hunting without gloves. As long as the weather permits I like not having gloves on so that I can pull the trigger of my gun quickly without having to remove gloves or mittens.

When the temperature gets colder I put on a pair of lightweight gloves, even in the very cold days. This is because the lightweight gloves can still usually be worn during shooting while they still provide some extra warmth.

If you plan on doing any hunting in the later times of the year then you will most likely want to have a nice pair of warm hunting gloves on. Similar to what we discussed with long underwear, still hunting while you wait for others to kick up pheasants will cause you to cool down faster because you are not moving around so having gloves on while you wait for pheasants to come out of hiding is a very good idea.

Boots

Lightweight boots, similar to hiking boots are very nice for the early season. If you are going to be actively going after pheasants you will want to be able to move quickly to keep up with these fast moving birds. Lightweight boots and active hiking/hunting shoes allow you to move quickly throughout the fields while still providing protection from stepping on branches, rocks etc…

Also, if you are wearing heavy hunting boots in warmer temperatures they can cause your feet to sweat and make for an uncomfortable hunt. However, there are times for warm winter hunting boots.

Grab your warm winter hunting boots for the cold days and for mild days that you will be doing a lot of still hunting waiting for others to scare pheasants to you. Having cold toes is one of biggest things that can turn a fun hunting adventure into a miserable experience.

Wool Socks

In the early season you can get away with just wearing regular socks. However, cold days may call for better warmth for your toes. Finding warm socks should be pretty easy. Go to your local sporting goods store and you can find wool socks at a reasonable price. Typically, you can get them for about $5-$10 a pair and they will be well worth the money to help keep your feet warm for the cold days.

Now let's examine licenses and hunter safety…

Step 2: Licensing & Hunter Safety

Get Your Small Game & Applicable Safety Registration

It is important to purchase a hunting license and learn hunting safety prior to heading out for a pheasant hunting adventure. The laws and regulations for hunting are very different from one area to the next. In the majority of cases you will need to purchase some type of hunting license to be able to hunt pheasants.

Additionally, you may also need to have some type of safety certification prior to purchasing a license. Ensure you have the proper license and safety before doing any type of hunting.

Legal Aspects to Consider Before Hunting

- Area you are hunting
- Specific hunting dates
- Bag limits
- Safety certification

Area

When you are going to purchase your hunting license the first thing you will need to know is what area you plan to hunt. Most pheasant hunting licenses are good for the entire state that you purchase the license in. If you will be hunting in multiple states than you will likely need multiple licenses.

Be aware that if you are not a resident of the state you plan to hunt in you will typically pay a higher rate for your license. Sometimes the increase is as much as double what it costs for a resident of that state to buy a license. If you are going to be hunting at a pheasant preserve you may luck out and not have to buy a license but again, check your local regulations first.

You should also consider what other type of hunting or fishing you plan to do within that year before you buy a hunting license. Some states allow you to purchase a type of combination license that will give you a combined hunting and fishing license for a discounted rate. Not only do you save a few dollars this way, it also helps reduce the amount of paperwork you need to carry around.

Hunting Dates

Not only do you need to know what areas you plan on hunting, you will also need to know the dates you plan on hunting pheasants. Most states sell their pheasant hunting licenses on a yearly basis. Sometimes the pheasant hunting is included with a small game license and sometimes you need to purchase an additional pheasant hunting stamp on top of your small game license.

Again, many times you buy a license it will be good for that hunting season. Perhaps September through December. When the next hunting season rolls around you will need to purchase another license and possibly pheasant hunting stamp.

Just be sure you understand the regulations to guarantee that you are covered during the dates that you plan to hunt. Unfortunately, not knowing the rules is not a good excuse if a game warden catches you without proper licensing. The penalties can be very harsh for people who violate the rules including loss of hunting privileges and confiscation of hunting equipment.

Bag Limits

The number of pheasants that you can legally shoot is something that you should be sure to understand prior to going pheasant hunting. Our hope is that you will have the opportunity to shoot many pheasants, just ensure you know when you must stop.

Bag limits will be listed in the hunting regulations booklet that you can get from any store that sells hunting licenses. In many areas you may find the limit to be 2-3 roosters per day that you can shoot.

Now you also need to be aware of possession limits associated with pheasants. A possession limit refers to the total number of pheasants that you can have at any given time. The easiest way to think of this is the number of pheasants that you have at your home at any one time.

A common possession limit is 3 times your daily bag limit. So if the bag limit in your area is 3 roosters then three times your bag limit is 9. That means that at any one time you can have 9 total pheasants in storage at your home.

Safety Certification

In addition to having proper licensing, you will also need to ensure that you obtain any necessary safety certifications prior to hunting pheasants.

Again, the rules in each area will vary widely. Some areas you will need to have a formal safety certification regardless of your age. In other areas if you are over a certain age you do not need to have safety training.

Even if your area does not require any safety training it is an excellent idea to go through a safety training course prior to doing any type of hunting. Although hunting can be a very fun activity it also comes with a certain level of safety risk.

You can never eliminate all risks when hunting but going through a formal safety class will teach you the skills to improve your safety practices. Hunting safety courses often range from $20-$100 for a few week course. This is a great investment in your long term safety.

Now let's examine gun types...

Step 3: Gun Types

Select from a Variety of Weapons for Hunting Pheasants

As with many types of hunting there is a large range of weapons to select from for hunting pheasants.

The one thing in common with all of the guns for pheasant hunting is that they are all shotguns. If you are not familiar what a shotgun is I am going to give you a quick overview. Essentially a shotgun is a gun that when fired it shoots many BBs out of a single shell. The number of BBs in a single shell will vary based on the shot size you select.

Shotguns are primarily used for bird hunting because it is the most effective way to hit birds that are flying. In contrast, a rifle is a gun that shoots a single bullet at one time. I think you can imagine that having a shotgun with a lot of BBs will have a much higher chance of hitting a bird in the air than a single bullet.

Although there are other weapons to use for hunting pheasant, we are going to cover the 4 most common types of shotgun used in pheasant hunting.

Guns for Pheasant Hunting:

- Pump Shotgun

- Semi Auto Shotgun

- Over Under Shotgun

- Side By Side Shotgun

Pump Shotgun

Pump shotguns are one of the most common types of shotguns. This is partially because they are going to be some of the most cost effective shotguns that you can find. If you are going to buy a new pump shotgun you might be able to get one for a few hundred dollars for an entry level gun. Of course you could spend much more if you want a gun with more features or you buy an expensive brand name gun.

The basic concept of a pump shotgun is that the gun reloads by a manual action that the hunter must make. There is a mechanism called a pump on the barrel of the gun that you pull back towards you after you shoot. This action loads the next shell into the chamber and the gun is then ready to take another shot.

Semi Auto Shotgun

Semi auto shotguns are also popular, particularly for people who also hunt waterfowl such as ducks and geese. The benefit of semi-auto shotguns is that there is no action required of the hunter to load the next round into the chamber. As soon as the hunter pulls the trigger to fire a round the gun automatically loads the next shell into the chamber.

This presents a huge advantage in the case of quick firing. With semi-auto shotguns you could shoot several rounds in just a few seconds, likely increasing your chances of bagging a pheasant.

However, the biggest downside of semi auto shotguns is the cost. Semi-auto shotguns brand new will start around $500 but in reality the majority of this style shotguns will be closer to $800 for a very basic model. If you are a person who also hunts ducks and geese this extra money might be worth the investment.

Over Under Shotgun

An over under shotgun is a type of shotgun that actually has two barrels, with one barrel stacked on top of the other barrel. This means that the gun will hold two rounds for shooting at pheasants.

The way some of these guns work is that you pull the trigger one time and it fires the first round and when you pull the trigger a second time it will fire the next round. Another way these guns operate is by having two triggers. You pull one trigger to shoot the shell from one barrel and then pull the other trigger to shoot from the other barrel.

To reload these guns they actually have a hinge by the chamber. After you shoot your two rounds you "break" the gun which means opening it at the hinge. Once it is open the two empty shells pop out and you put in two unfired shells.

Side By Side Shotgun

Side by side shotguns are very similar in function to over under shotguns. Side by side shotguns have two barrels next to each other rather than stacked on top of each other. Again these will either be fired by pulling one trigger two times to shoot both rounds or some styles have two separate triggers.

Finally, the side by side shotguns load similar to over under shotguns. You "break" the gun at the hinge area and you load in two more rounds to shoot at pheasants.

Now let's take a look at gun accessories that you may want to consider...

Step 4: Additional Firearm Considerations

What are the additional considerations that go along with your firearm?

The most obvious consideration that you will need for your gun is the shells but there are many other items that you should consider for pheasant hunting.

What to consider:

- Shot Size

- Shell Length/Chamber Size

- Gauge

- Barrel Length

Shot Size

The shells you select will play a role in your pheasant hunting success. There are large variety of shotgun shells that you can choose from as you go pheasant hunting. Over time you will see what you prefer but here will give you some general recommendations.

The shot size of your shell refers to the size of the BBs that are in each shell.

Shot sizes for pheasant hunting (smallest to largest BB size):

- 8

- 7 ½

- 7

- 6 shot

- 4 shot

- 2 shot

Keep in mind, the larger shot size you choose that fewer BB than can fit in a shell. For example, a 4 shot shell will have more BBs than the 2 shot.

The advantage of more BB is you get a larger kill radius because there are more BBs in the air to hit your target. The downside is that they have less killing power than larger pellets, particularly for larger birds.

Ultimately, any of these shot sizes will work if you have an accurately placed shot at a very short range but if you want the most recommended shotgun shell type I would suggest that you start with 4 or 6 shot for most pheasant hunting situations.

Shell Length/Chamber Size

Typical shotgun shells range in length from 2 ½ inches to 3 ½ inches. The larger the shell size typically the more range and kill power.

Shell length options:

- 2 ½ inch

- 2 ¾ inch

- 3 inch

- 3 ½ inch

2 ¾ and 2 ½ inches are the most common for hunting small game, including pheasants. The primary reason is you are usually taking pretty close shots so there is really no need to shoot 3 inch or 3 ½ inch shells.

The other consideration with shooting the 2 ¾ and 2 ½ inch shells is you will notice a cost difference as you go up in shell length. You can expect to pay about $5 more per box for 3 inch shells compared to 2 3/4 inch shells.

When you buy your shotgun or you look to borrow one to try out pheasant hunting you should pay attention to the chamber size. The chamber size will correlate with what shell length that you can use.

For example a gun that has a 2 ½ inch chamber will not hold shells that are larger than 2 ½ inch such as a 3 inch shell. In contrast, a shotgun with a 3 ½ inch chamber will typically handle any shotgun shell that is smaller. Basically if you have a gun with a 3 ½ inch chamber you could hold pretty much any size shotgun shell.

Gauge

With shotguns, the gauge refers to the size of the bore or essentially how big in diameter and powerful of a shogun shell load it holds. The lower the gauge size the more powerful the gun. For example, a 20 gauge shotgun is less powerful than a 12 gauge shotgun.

The downside of more powerful shotguns is they have stronger recoil or kick when you shoot them. If you are doing a lot of shooting in a given day your shoulders can get sore from the recoil of each shot.

The standard shotgun for pheasant hunting is a 12 gauge and these are very effective in most situations. If you are a youth or smaller sized hunter then 20 gauge shotguns can work. They will not have quite as much power but they are typically light enough for the majority of smaller hunters to be able to handle the weight and recoil.

Barrel Length

The barrel length of shotguns refers to the length of the barrel that extends beyond the primary workings of the shotguns. Typically longer barrels will keep the shot pattern tighter for further distances. This means that your shots can be effective for longer distances.

However, the downside of longer barrel length is that they can be difficult to carry through thick brush and add weight to your gun.

The most common sized barrels for pheasant shotguns are 26, 28 and 30 inches. My preference is a 28 inch barrel as they versatile if you hunt other game such as ducks, geese or grouse.

Now let's discuss what else you should consider bringing with on your hunt…

Step 5: What Else to Bring Hunting

Bring these Items to Prepare for Hunting Pheasants

Now that we have discussed weapon types and gun accessories, let's take a look at some of the other items that you may want to bring with you on your hunting trip.

What else should I bring with hunting?

- Hunting knife

- Compass

- Vest with game pocket

- Food & water

Hunting Knife

A hunting knife is one of the most important items that you will want to bring with on your outdoor adventure. After you shoot a pheasant you will need a knife to be able to clean your pheasant. You will remove the guts and skin of the pheasant and usually the best place to leave the guts is in the woods. We will discuss how to clean your pheasant with a hunting knife in an upcoming section.

Make sure that you sharpen your knife before you go as a sharp knife makes cutting easier. Surprisingly a sharp knife adds to your safety because you won't have to push so hard to cut which will reduce the chances of the knife slipping and cutting yourself.

Compass

Depending on the area you are going to hunt and how framilar you are with the woods you are in it can be a great idea to bring a compass with. In most cases, the areas that I hunt I know the land extremely well and don't bring a compass.

However, anytime that you are hunting a new area that you have never been to before you sould bring a compass for safety. The chances of getting lost are pretty slim but it is better to have one with to be safe.

In addition to bringing a seperate compass, many smart phones now have compases either installed on them from the factory or you can get an application that will serve as a compass. This is a nice feature so you do not need to go out and buy a compass.

The only downside with this is you need to be sure that your phone is charged and that you will be an area that has cell phone service as many times these apps only work when there is reception.

Vest With Game Pocket

We discussed clothing in an earlier section but one piece of clothing that is very convenient is a hunting vest with a game pocket. These vest types are often seen on pheasant hunters and are also great for all small game hunting.

Basically, these are hunting vests that have a pouch on the back side that allows you to place game that you shoot in for storage. Hopefully you will shoot several pheasants when you are hunting so it good to have a way to carry them while you walk through the woods and look for more pheasants or while you are walking home.

Without a vest you may end up carrying the pheasants you shoot by the legs which can be a pretty easy way to carry them but the problem is if you see another pheasant your hands will be full. Then you have to set the pheasants down and take the time to come back and find them after you chase down the next pheasant.

If you do not have a vest then you could consider bringing a backpack. Use a backpack that you do not care if it gets dirty as it will get very dirty and I would not recommend using it for anything besides hunting after you have put pheasants in it.

Food & Water

It is never a bad idea to bring some water and a few snacks with on your hunting trip. When you are going to go hunting for just an hour or so a bottle of water and a snack bar should get you through. Having just this little bit of food and water can help keep you hydrated and energized.

When you plan longer trips you may want to bring a few bottles of water and even pack a lunch. Without food and water it may cause you to have to go back sooner than you want. With some food you can extend your hunting trip, particularly on those days when you are having good success.

Now let's find out where to hunt…

Step 6: Where to Hunt

How to Select the Proper Location to Hunt Pheasants

Finding good hunting spots can help you improve your chances of success with pheasant hunting. Let's take a look at some places to go pheasant hunting.

Identifying Areas for Pheasant Hunting:

- Pay attention to where you see pheasants

- Fields

- Areas near standing water and marshes

- Near barns and corn cribs

- By farm machinery and other equipment

Pay Attention to Where you See Pheasants

This should be obvious but you want to pay attention to where you see pheasants. When you are driving around keep an eye out in the fields and woods and actively look for pheasants. If you often see pheasants in a certain area this should be a great place for you to start.

Also, you can ask your friends and family to be on the lookout for you. Let them know that you want to go pheasant hunting and ask if they could pay attention to what they are seeing. It is better to have several people searching for pheasants rather than just you and often time's friends and family will be willing to help you out with this.

Another strategy to get the feedback of others on good places to hunt is to make a posting to your favorite social media website and let everyone know that you are looking to go pheasant hunting and ask if any of your friends have suggestions on where to go. This is a great way to get the word out to a lot of people at once and often people will be willing to help you out and provide some ideas.

Fields

Like many animals, pheasants like easy to find food sources so they will often live near a field that has crops such corn, alfalfa and a variety of other plants. Pheasants will then have a great food resource for several months out of the year as the crops grow and even after the fields are harvested.

Now it is not always possible to see pheasants in the fields because if the crops are still standing there is really no way to see them in the field. For example, corn fields are usually 4-5 feet tall and pheasants are just a foot or two tall when standing.

Even if you do not see pheasants in the corn fields as long as you are in an area that you have seen some pheasants it will likely be worth your time to walk through the fields in order to attempt to kick up some pheasants. We will discuss the strategies on how to walk through fields for pheasants in depth later on.

Woods

Hunting for pheasants can also be done inside of woods and the edges of heavily wooded areas. This is because pheasants will travel through the woods and they like all of the hiding spots that a woods provides.

The significant downside that woods have for you as the hunter is the fact that pheasants have a lot of spots to hide and even if you are able to scare them up there will likely be branches and leaves in the way as you try and shoot them. This does not mean that hunting in woods is a bad idea it just means that you will have to pay particular attention to shooting lanes in order to hit pheasants in these situations.

Brush

Similar to hunting pheasants in fields, pheasants like to hide in brush and it is an excellent place to attempt to find pheasants. Brush alongside road ditches, near woods and nearly every other place that you have a sizeable section of brush can make a great spot to try and find pheasants.

Areas Near Standing Water and Marshes

All animals need to drink water eventually so areas near standing water and marshes are prime spots to find pheasants. In addition to having water, these areas usually have a lot of cover that they provide for the birds so they like to hide out there.

The downside is that you will need to trudge through some very difficult terrain to get to the pheasants in the marshes. Here is a time that you will want to have waterproof knee boots or even waders depending on how much standing water there is in the area.

Near Barns and Corn Cribs

Along the same subject of being near fields with standing crops, pheasants really like it when they do not need to go to a field for food. Many crop farmers use some type of silo or corn crib to hold their harvested crops. This is truly a pheasants dream. An open corn crib is stuffed full of food that could feed a group of pheasants for months.

When I go hunting one of the first places I check is near the corn crib because there is usually at least one pheasant in the area. If there is not one currently feeding on the crops, there is still likely to be one very close by.

Just put yourself in the mind of a pheasant and how you would want to stay to your food source as place to live. If you find their food source then you are more than likely to find some pheasants.

Near Farm Equipment and other Machinery

Another prime location to find pheasants is near farm equipment and other machinery. Often time's farmers leave some equipment out in their yard or pasture. Sometimes this equipment has been there for years and the equipment now has tall grass growing around it.

This is a prime spot for pheasants because of the excellent source of cover these machines create as well as they are likely close to some type of food source.

Now let's discuss how to get permission to hunt private land...

Step 7: How to Get Permission to Hunt Private Land

For Non-Landowners, here are some tips.

If you are like me, you do not own hunting land and do not want to battle other hunters for public land. If this is your situation then you will need to get permission to hunt private land.

At first it can feel a little uncomfortable to ask other people to use their land to hunt on. However, after some experience the process gets much easier. Also, if you get permission to hunt on land from someone they are pretty likely to let you come back again in the future.

How to Get Permission to Hunt Private Land?

- Don't be afraid to ask

- Don't wear hunting clothes

- Be kind and smile

- Bring a youth hunter if possible

- Tell them exact times you will be there

- Do a favor in return

- Bring them meat or another gift

- Thank them after

Don't Be Afraid to Ask

Something that holds hunters back from getting land to hunt is the fear of asking for permission. People can feel intimidated by asking landowners for permission and I shared the same fear when I first began asking for permission to hunt private land but the more you do it the more you get used to asking.

When you are turned down the primary reason is that they already have a friend or family member that hunts the area. I have never had anyone get upset at me for asking.

Example Wording to Use

To help you get started here are a few phrases to try:

- Hello, my name is Scott and I am hoping to hunt to do some pheasant hunting tomorrow. It seems like you have a great piece of land for pheasant hunting. Would it be ok with you if I hunted on your property this weekend?

- Good afternoon, I am looking for a place to pheasant hunt with my daughter tomorrow. Would it be possible for us to hunt on your land for pheasants for a few hours in the afternoon?

- Hello, I was driving by and I saw several pheasants on your property. I really enjoy pheasant hunting and I'm wondering if it would be ok with you if I could hunt here for a few hours today?

- If they say no, don't waste this opportunity to find a hunting spot. Say "Thank you, I understand. Do you happen to know of any other places nearby that you would suggest that I try?" They might know another landowner that would allow you to hunt nearby or they might know of some good public land for hunting in the area.

Don't Wear Hunting Clothing

I recommend not wearing hunting clothing when you go to ask for permission to hunt because it can give the landowners a feeling that you are assuming that you will be able to hunt there. Not all people like or allow hunting so don't add this element of hunting to your first interaction with the landowner.

If you are planning on hunting that same day at least take off your orange hat and hunting vest. It should not take too much to remove the items that make you look like a hunter. Again, it is better to error on the side of not looking like a hunter because sometimes it can also give them the impression that you may go hunt in their land even if they do not give you permission.

Be Kind and Smile

This should go without saying but if you are polite to the landowner they will more than likely be polite back. Be conscious when you approach the property to put a smile on your face to ensure that you are received as a friendly individual.

Be sure to put off an energy about yourself that you are friendly and easy to get along with. Do what you can to strike up a conversation with the landowner by asking them how long they have lived at the property and what they do for a living. People love to talk about themselves so if you can get the conversation going and let the landowner talk it will likely improve your chances of getting permission to hunt their land.

If they allow you to hunt, keep the conversation going and ask them where they would recommend hunting. After all, they should know best where the pheasants will be on their property.

Bring a Youth Hunter

Most people have a soft spot for children and if you are planning on hunting with a child it can help to bring them with as you ask for permission. People who would have said no to you alone may say yes if it means that a child will get the opportunity to experience the outdoors.

Another benefit of bringing a child is that it can be a great learning experience for the child. This helps get the child used to speaking to strangers and all of the aspects of hunting that will be valuable to them when they start hunting on their own.

Tell Them the Exact Times You will be There

To help put the landowners at ease it is important to let them know exactly when you plan to hunt. If you want to hunt just one morning tell them that or if you want an entire weekend be specific so they are not taken off guard when they see people on their property.

I think this is very important because people will feel more comfortable knowing the exact times that they could expect to see you rather than having you show up at any random time of the day. Maybe they have friends or family coming over for a visit and if they do they are able to tell their visitors this information so you not take someone off guard when you show up to do some hunting.

Never go during a time where you do not have permission.

Do a Favor In Return

Landowners often have work that needs to be done around their property, particularly if they are farmers. Ask them if there are a few projects that you could help out with for an afternoon or two in exchange for getting hunting permission.

Not only would assisting with these chores be a way get permission to hunt, it is also a great way to form a relationship with the landowner. The more you get to know them the more likely they are to let you to continue to hunt there.

Bring them Meat or Other Small Gifts

Another thing you can do is to ask if the landowners would like to get meat in exchange for allowing you to hunt. Even if they don't hunt people may like having some free meat. This can be a great win-win situation for both parties.

Not all people like pheasant meat so you could bring some other type of small gift as a way to say thank you to the landowner for allowing you to use their property. You could bake some cookies in advance or stop at the store on the way and buy some cookies to give them.

It does not have to be anything very expensive but something simple can go a long way in letting them know that you appreciate their generosity of allowing you to hunt on their property.

Benefits of Getting Permission Effectively

If you follow these steps and you are respectful with those who allow you to hunt their land you may end up with a long term hunting spot.

Be kind when asking, do something in return and get to know those landowners. The better connections you make with people the more likely you will build a great network of hunting locations that you can use.

Our next section covers finding public land for pheasant hunting…

Step 8: Finding Public Land to Hunt

Public Land Can Provide Excellent Hunting Opportunities

Similar to private land, with a little effort you can find some great hunting spots available on public land.

What types of public lands are available for hunting?

- WMAs or Wildlife Management Areas

- State Forests

- Wildlife Refuges

- National Forests

- County Land

- and many more…

Tips about Public Land

- Contact your state wildlife office

- Scout the area in advance

- Safety

Contact Your State Wildlife Office

With a little online research you will be sure to find some public hunting land within a reasonable driving distance from your home. Simply search for any of the above terms online followed by your state or county name and there will be a listing.

Each state has different regulations for these areas so if you have questions regarding hunting regulations that are not clearly outlined online be sure to reach out to your state wildlife office directly.

State wildlife officers are usually very friendly people and passionate about the outdoors. When you call the wildlife office do not be afraid to ask them what areas they would suggest nearby for you to try pheasant hunting. They want to help people enjoy the outdoors so if you ask, they are going to be happy to assist.

Scout the Area in Advance

If possible it is great to scout the area in advance. Try driving to the hunting location a few days in advance and review the territory. You can do this by talking a walk through the fields and woods and make note of where you see pheasants.

Even if you are unable to physically go to the hunting spot in advance you can use online resources to help you plan your hunt. Since you may have found this location by looking online for public hunting areas you can usually find online maps for these public lands as well.

Scan those maps and see where the fields are and other nearby open areas and woods etc. This will help you plan your walking path in advance and hopefully help you improve your chances of success.

Safety

Safety is the primary thing to be aware of when hunting on public land. Since it is public land, anyone can use this land and there is not any way to guarantee that you are alone in the woods.

You need to ensure that you are wearing proper hunting attire that we discussed earlier. In most cases this means wearing blaze orange on the top ½ of your body. By doing this it will allow other hunters to see you more easily.

Additionally, it is important to check your surroundings before you shoot. It can be easy to get caught up in the excitement of shooting at a pheasant that you forget to check what is around you. However, you want to think about what is behind the area that you are shooting at as bullets can travel a long distance and you need to be 100% sure that there is nobody in the direction that you are shooting.

If you are ever in doubt if you are taking a safe shot do not shoot.

Now let's discuss how you can prepare for your hunt...

Step 9: Prepping for Your Hunt

A little prep time goes a long way for a successful hunt

Before you head out for your hunt, ensure you are fully prepared for a fun outdoor adventure. If you want to be sure you have everything you need for a successful trip you might even consider making yourself a checklist that you can use before each trip.

What should you do to prepare for your hunt?

- Inspect all equipment & guns

- Purchase ammo & licenses

- Checklist of items before leaving

Inspect all Equipment & Guns

It is very important to inspect all of your hunting equipment including your guns before going out hunting. Sharpen your hunting knives and make sure all of your clothes are in good condition.

It is also important to ensure your guns are in proper working order. With any gun it is a good idea to shoot a few rounds prior to the hunting season to ensure everything is in working order and it is shooting accurately.

I also like to clean out my guns before I go hunting. Proper gun care involves thoroughly cleaning them a few times throughout the season and again before you put your guns away for the year. So even though I would have cleaned my gun at the end of the previous season, I will be sure to clean it as I get everything ready for the next season in case any dust or other items settled on my gun during storage.

While we are on the subject of cleaning guns I would like to share with you one of the best cleaning tools that I have come across. It is called a bore snake and they are made to clean out the barrel of your gun. They typically cost about $20 and are very easy to use. Bore snakes are about 10 inches long and on one end they have a 20 inch rope with a metal piece that you drop into the end of your barrel. The rope comes out of the other end of the barrel and you simply grab the rope and pull then entire unit through your barrel.

As the bore snake moves through your barrel there are tiny bristles and fabric that help collect and clean out any dirt and gunpowder residue. You simply run the bore snake through your barrel 2 or 3 times and it is clean. This is much faster than using a rod with cleaning swabs attached to the end.

Purchase Ammo & Licenses

You will want to ensure you have all of your licenses purchased in advance. We discussed licenses earlier but it is worth mentioning again to avoid any illegal hunting. Additionally, there are often cut off dates for buying licenses. Even if there are not cut off dates many areas have a waiting period where it takes 1-2 days for a purchased license to become effective. This is to prevent people shooting a pheasant and then going directly to a store to buy the license.

Having ammo on hand is also important. The good thing about ammunition is it really does not expire, at least for many, many years. For people who hunt in remote areas it is even more important to have enough ammo because you cannot easily get to a store to purchase more. Error on the side of having extra ammo as you can always save the left over for the next year.

Checklist of Items Before Leaving

Taking a little time to create a checklist of all of the items you will need on your hunting trip is a great way to ensure that you are prepared for an enjoyable hunt. Before you leave on your hunting trip double-check your list to make sure nothing is missed.

Do you have your ammunition? Do you have a compass? Do you have your knife? All of these are critical items to ensure that you are ready for a fun day of pheasant hunting. I can tell you from experience that it will quickly put a damper on your hunting trip if you forget one of these critical items.

For example, one time I forgot that I had the safety trigger lock on my gun. I realized this after I had already driven ½ hour to my hunting spot. Unfortunately I did not have the key with to take the lock off my trigger so my gun was useless at that point. It was so frustrating to have spent so much time getting prepared but then I forgot something so simple. Do yourself a favor and create a basic checklist to ensure this does not happen to you.

Now let's look at the different seasons for pheasant hunting...

Step 10: Hunting Seasons

Enjoy the Challenges and Opportunities Created By Each Season

Every season provides uniqueness for hunting pheasants. This is one thing that keeps this sport fun and exciting because no matter what time of year you go you will find new opportunities and challenges to overcome.

Let's take a look at the seasons for pheasant hunting and what they provide for hunting excitement.

Seasons:

- Early Season

- Mid-Season

- Late Season

Early Season

Typical early season starting dates for pheasant hunting are late September to the middle of October. One clear benefit of hunting during the early season is the temperature. Regardless of where you are located this time of year will usually have some warm to moderate temperatures.

You could actually be hunting in 70 and 80 degree temperatures in the early season which would be quite comfortable for hunting. However, if you are going to be active hunting for pheasants you might actually get too warm.

After going 6 months or more without hunting, it can be so exciting to rush out to the fields, woods and prairies to hunt on opening day of pheasant hurting. I have found myself rushing out to the fields as well and love to get the early hunting in to scratch my itch for hunting pheasants.

However, the early season will present a huge challenge in regards to visibility of pheasants. Leaves, brush, branches and more will still all be on the trees and ground and these will create difficult hunting situations. Also, most all of the crops will still be standing during the early season, again creating a lot of cover for pheasants. During this time of year a pheasant on the ground in the woods be challenging to see, much less shoot successfully.

Mid-Season

As the year progresses it becomes easier to see pheasants on the ground. The months of late October and November are when the majority of the shrubs and brush on the ground will thin out and more fields with crops have been harvested which will help create more clear visibility of pheasants. To be successful in hunting pheasants you need to be able to see them so the mid-season is often one of the best times of year to shoot pheasants.

Another benefit of the mid-season is that the temperatures can still be pretty mild but not too cold where you will be uncomfortable for hunting. In fact, having cooler temperatures will be nice if you plan to active hunt pheasants where you move through the fields at a quick pace. The cooler temperatures will help keep you naturally cool.

Late Season

The late season is usually November and December and will present significantly lower temperatures. In addition to the lower temperatures, you may also have to deal with snow.

To deal with these temperatures ensure that you dress appropriately with thicker coats and winter boots. During this time of year you will have the benefit of very clear areas in the woods free of leaves and vegetation on the ground to see pheasants.

Tracking is another benefit of hunting in the late season when there is snow on the ground. Snow makes it very easy to see tracks on the ground. You can follow tracks to where the pheasants have gone to and try to find pheasants.

What is the best time of day for hunting…

Step 11: Time of Day for Pheasant Hunting

Use Pheasant Behavior to Your Benefit

The good news is that pheasants can be hunted at pretty much any time of day so don't be discouraged if you cannot get out hunting in the first ½ hour of daylight.

In this section we will discuss the times of day and how each can be effective for pheasant hunting:

- Morning
- Afternoon
- Evening
- Pheasant hunting as a time filler for other hunting

Mornings

Taking advantage of the morning feeding time is an excellent way to bag some pheasants. As the sun comes up in the morning the pheasants begin to get off their resting spots and head out to feed.

Now you need to check your local regulations on when you can begin hunting pheasants in the morning. For example, in Minnesota the legal hunting time does not start until 9am so be sure to keep an eye on the clock before you start hunting in the morning.

If you are actively hunting for pheasants first thing in the morning the chances are that you will get some excellent hunting opportunities. Check the areas that are on the side of fields and pastures as the pheasants may be grazing on grass and other vegetation. You should also check near the water in your area. Check near the edges of those ponds to see if any pheasants are nearby.

Afternoon

It is possible to have pheasant hunting success during the entire day. In fact, some of my best pheasant hunting trips have been in the afternoon. If you only have a small amount of time to go pheasant hunting and it happens to be in the afternoon that will be just fine.

The afternoons also have great visibility due to the sun being higher in the sky so you can pick out the pheasants easier. You also get to enjoy the warmer temperature of the afternoon compared to cooler temps in the morning and evening.

Evening

Evening hunts refer to the last hour or two of sunlight. Check your local regulations to see how late into the evening you can hunt legally. Similar to the morning, pheasants come out during this time to feed.

Since pheasants will be feeding they will be out in the pastures, fields and woods which should allow you a good chance of seeing a pheasant and hopefully getting a chance of shooting one. In my opinion the last ½ hour of sunlight is one of the absolute best times to find pheasants out and in a good spot to be able to shoot.

Pheasant Hunting as a Filler for Other Hunting

Tracking through the fields for pheasants is a great way to pass some extra time when you are doing other hunting for other animals. So even though first thing in the morning and the last ½ hour of daylight are very good for producing results do not be afraid to hunt whenever you have time.

As an example, I hunt for ducks and geese and the prime time for them is the first few hours of the morning. We will get our fill of ducks and geese and before we are ready to leave for the day we take ½ hour to walk the areas for pheasants.

I really enjoy the extra variety that it adds to my hunting day. Additionally, it helps extend the hunting day as the ducks and geese in my area become very hard to come by after about 10am.

Now we will take a look at how to identify pheasants...

Step 12: Identifying Pheasant

Learn the various types of pheasants before hunting

It is extremely important to know what type of pheasant you are shooting at before you pull the trigger. Depending on your area and the license you purchased you may only be able to shoot certain types of pheasants.

In fact, many areas only allow you to shoot the male pheasants which are called roosters. Due to this fact it is very critical that you know how to identify the differences between the two kinds of pheasants.

Common Types of Pheasant:

- Rooster
- Hen

Rooster

The rooster is the male ring neck pheasant. The good news is that male pheasants are very colorful compared to the females so it is pretty easy to tell the difference between the two types of pheasants.

Males have gold/copper feathers on their sides, red faces with purple head feathers and a very distinguishable white ring around its neck. The roosters are also known for their loud cackling sound that you can hear from a long distance away. Many times when you kick up a rooster pheasant they will make this cackling noise as well allowing you to not only verify their type with color but also sound.

As we discussed already, most areas only allow you to shoot roosters so you need to be sure that you identify the pheasant before you pull the trigger. If you are ever in doubt if it is a rooster that you are shooting at it is best to hold off on pulling the trigger. You are better off trying to find your next pheasant rather than shooting a hen on accident.

Hen

In stark contrast to the rosters, hens are very plain in their color. First off, hens are the female breed of pheasants. Hens are primarily brown in color and have some black feathers throughout their bodies.

You will also notice that the hens have much shorter tail feathers compared to the roosters. Also, the hens do not make the loud cackling that you hear from the roosters so you can be sure if the pheasant is cackling it is not a hen.

Now let's examine how to find signs of pheasants…

Step 13: Looking for Signs of Pheasants

Pay Attention to Locate Pheasants

A key to successfully hunting for pheasants is to try and find a place with signs of pheasants in the area. If you find some of these signs then it is likely that you will be able to find pheasants nearby.

Common Signs of Pheasants in the Area:

- Footprints
- Droppings (i.e. poop)
- Rooster cackling

Footprints

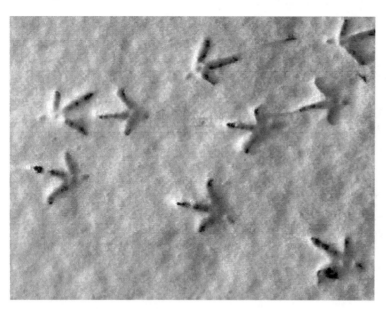

One way to know that pheasants are in the area is by the footprints they leave behind. However, depending on the time of year that you are hunting it can be challenging to find pheasant footprints because of hard dirt and leaves that they walk on. There is not always mud or snow to leave behind their tracks.

Hunting for pheasants in the snow will be one of the best times to be able to see where pheasants are traveling from the footprints they leave behind. Their footprints will vary in size based on the size of the pheasant. As an example, pheasants are some of the largest pheasants that you will find so the footprints for this pheasant type will be larger.

You will also notice the footprint pattern of the pheasant to be somewhat different from other animals. This pattern difference is due to the way that pheasants hop as they run. There will be the two front paw prints but then you will see the two rear leg prints closer together forming somewhat of a triangle pattern. The pattern should be fairly easy to pick out compared to the other animal prints you might see in your hunting area.

Droppings

Another indicator of pheasants in the area is their droppings. Most pheasant droppings are about 1 inch across, tube shaped and 3-4 inches long. You will usually see a pile of these in one place that a pheasant went to the bathroom. Typically a pile of about 5-10 or more is what you will see.

As you walk through fields woods be sure to take time to not only observe the ground for prints but also look to see droppings on the ground. If you do find a pile of droppings you can stop to examine them for a moment.

If you look at the droppings and they have a wet appearance than that means that the droppings are fresh and that the pheasants were in the area recently. When the droppings have a dried out appearance that means they are old and this might be a spot that pheasants were using but have now moved on from.

Pheasant Cackling

Rooster pheasants make a cackling sound and you can hear this sound from a long ways away. If you hear this off in the distance you should try and get close to the area you heard the rooster. Sometimes they will keep making the sound but more often than not it will be done intermittently.

Let's examine some ways to hunt pheasants...

Step 14: Stocking Pheasant

Actively Walking to Find Pheasants can Produce Great Results

Stocking for Pheasant means that you walk through fields and woods to actively find pheasants. Who can think of a better way to have fun outdoors while getting some exercise?

In this section we will discuss the strategies on how to do this best if you are hunting by yourself, in a later section we will look at some ways to party hunt with many other hunters and even with the assistance of dogs.

Critical Components to Pheasant Stocking:

- Plan your route
- Make noise to Kick Up Pheasants
- Stop often and observe

- Always be ready to shoot
- Move quickly when you see pheasants in the distance

Plan Your Route

As you get ready to actively hunt for pheasants by yourself it is important to plan your route. You should think about the area you are going to be hunting and try and strategize what the best way will be to cover all of the area in the most effective manner.

For example, if it is a small field maybe you walk down ½ of the field and when you get to one end you turn around and walk back down the other ½ of the field. Maybe you are hunting larger field then you could try to zig-zag through the field and eventually get from one side of the field to the other and cover as much ground as possible.

You should also think about what the high traffic areas will likely be for pheasants. Areas near fields and other food sources are places that you should be sure to check. Additionally, areas near water can be effective as the pheasants will eventually need to drink water.

Make Noise to Kick Up Pheasants

As you actively hunt for pheasants it is best to try and make noise to kick them up off their resting spots. This can feel contradictory compared to other hunting where you want to be as quiet as possible.

However, with pheasant hunting you want to scare the pheasants up so that you can shoot at them in the air. When pheasants are on the ground they are going to be nearly impossible to see and that is why you need to get them up flying for your best chances of shooting them.

While you walk shout words like "UP", "GET UP", or just simply yell. Really the words you use are not important it is just important that you make some type of noise to get the pheasants moving. Yelling may seem silly at first but if you are motivated to shoot pheasants then you will quickly get over this feeling.

Stop Often and Observe

To ensure you have the best chances of seeing and hearing pheasants you will want to stop every 5-10 steps and actively look around. When you are walking it is hard to hear pheasants because of the amount of noise you make while walking but when you stop it should get much quieter.

Listen closely for anything that may sound like a pheasant. When you are hunting in a woods you can often hear them walking through the woods as they step on leaves and as branches crack that they happen to step on.

In addition to listening, you should also scan your surroundings. Be particularly aware of any movement that you see and watch that area closely to see if it was a pheasant. If you think you saw something move, ensure you give it a few moments before you move because they will usually resume moving shortly.

Now one trick to use when you are hunting in a field of standing corn or other crops is to look down the rows. As an example, corn is planted in rows so it will be easiest for you as the hunter to just walk straight down one row of corn. However, you may never see a pheasant that is running down the row of corn that is right next to you unless you check.

What you want to do is zig-zag from one row to the next every 10-15 steps and look down the rows of corn. Let's say the field of corn is small and it is 50 rows of corn wide, well you should take time to move back and forth as you make your way through the field to look through as many rows as possible. This way you can have a better chance of seeing any pheasants that are running down the corn rows.

Always be Ready to Shoot

When walking through fields and woods you should keep your gun in a position that allows you to quickly get into shooting position. Have the stock of the gun in one hand and the other hand near the base of the barrel where you normally hold your gun when shooting.

Holding your gun in this manner will allow you to get your gun in a shooting position very quickly if you kick up a pheasant. The key with pheasant hunting is that the quicker you are able to make your shots the better. This is because the pheasants will quickly put distance between you and them and the closer the bird is when you shoot the better your chances are at hitting the bird and the more dropping power your BBs will have.

However, be careful to pay attention to safety when you are walking with a loaded gun. Always be sure to keep the barrel pointed away from any other hunters and yourself. When you are traveling over logs and other difficult terrain you need to further increase your safety awareness.

Move Quickly When you see Pheasants in the Distance

When I see pheasants off in the distance I will move as quickly as possible to get close to where they are. Pheasants can move very fast through fields and ground so if you do not get to where they are quickly then you will likely lose out on the opportunity to shoot them.

Again, it is important to keep safety in mind as you move through fields and woods quickly. First, you want to ensure that your gun is on safe and that if you happen to trip that the gun is not pointed in the direction of another hunter, yourself or any buildings.

You also want to be aware of any tripping hazards such as downed branches or fences. Of course if you are hunting an area you are very familiar with you should have a good idea of where the fences are but a tree could have fallen down in the path since the last time that you hunting the area.

Now let's discuss party hunting for pheasants…

Step 15: Party Hunting for Pheasants

Group Hunting With Friends Can Produce Excellent Results

"Party" hunting for pheasants refers to more than one hunter pursuing pheasants. In addition to the significantly increased chances of successfully hunting pheasants this provides, party hunting also provides the opportunity for spending time with friends and relatives in the outdoors.

As an individual hunter it is very difficult to cover a large field by yourself. Even if you use the zig zagging method there is still plenty of opportunity for the pheasants to be elusive and they can sometimes move back and forth through the rows of crops while you do always working to stay out of your sight. However, with the assistance of many other hunters, it is much more difficult for the pheasants to stay out of sight.

Strategies and benefits of Party Hunting for Pheasants

- Pushing out fields and tall grass
- Pushing out woods
- Flushing pheasants from parked machinery & hiding spots

- Shared bag limits
- Company

Pushing out Fields and Tall Grass

One of the absolute best ways to party hunt pheasants is to push out large fields or areas of tall grass. In these cases the more hunters you have the better as you will be able to cover more of the field which will reduce the chances that pheasants will go undetected or be able to fly away without a hunter in close enough shooting distance.

Drive Example:

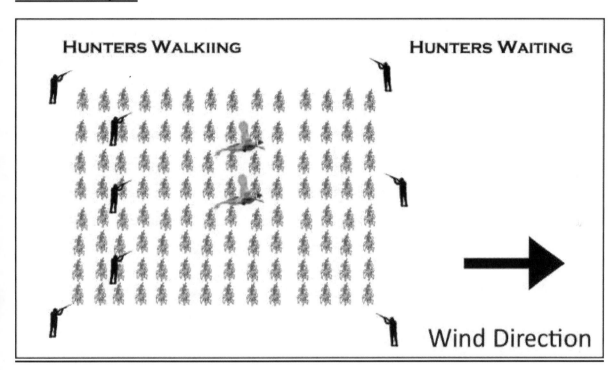

As the above diagram illustrates, we are hunting a large field that is square in shape. The first thing you want to do is determine the direction that the wind is going. In this case the wind is blowing from left to right.

What this means is that that we want our hunters who will be walking through the field to start on the far left side and walk to the right. This is because as they walk through the field the wild will blow the scent of the hunters towards any pheasants in the field to scare them up.

Before any hunters start walking in the field you want to setup your waiting hunters. In this picture there are the hunters that are stationed at the far right of the field. The job of these hunters is to stay standing in this position and wait for the hunters walking through the field to kick up pheasants towards them. As you can see, any pheasants that are in the fields will likely fly right over the top of these hunters and should make it pretty easy for the standing hunters to shoot.

After you have your standing hunters positioned you will also want to leave a few hunters behind if possible. In this picture these are the hunters at the far left of the image. Now this is not a critical piece of pheasant hunting but if you have plenty of hunters then I would recommend doing this. The reason you would leave a few hunters behind is if a pheasant gets kicked up by the walking hunters and circles back. This way any pheasants that do this will be easily shot by the left behind hunters.

Finally, you will want all remaining hunters to get ready to walk through the field. You will want the hunters to spread out as evenly as possible in the field to cover as much ground as possible. In the picture above we have 3 hunters so each of them is responsible for covering 1/3 of the field as they walk.

Now as the hunters walk they should make as much noise as possible. We discussed this in earlier sections but they should yell "UP" or "GET UP" or really anything they want but the intent is to make sure that the pheasants can hear them so they get scared and start flying.

The walking hunters will also want to zig zag as they cover their 1/3 of the field. They should take about 10-15 steps and then move to the next row of corn. They will continue to do this to try as much ground as possible for their 1/3 of the field. As they zig zag they should be looking down each of the rows of corn to see if there are any pheasants running.

When party hunting like this be sure to take turns so each hunter has some opportunities to shoot pheasants. Typically the hunters who are stationed at the far end of the field waiting for birds to fly over are the hunters who get the most shooting in.

Pushing Out Woods

When you are hunting with a party you have the advantage to push out woods and brush. This will be done in a very similar manner to what we just described in the above diagram for pushing out a field.

You should always start with having some hunters stationed at all corners of the woods or brush so as the walking hunters move through the woods the standing hunters will have clear opportunities to shoot any approaching pheasants.

For example, if you have 6 hunters you could have 3 of the hunters walking through the woods doing their best to make noise and kick up pheasants while the other 3 are positioned in strategic spots surrounding the woods to shoot the pheasants as they come out of hiding.

When you do this style of hunting be sure that you trade off roles regularly so all hunters all get an equal opportunity to shoot some pheasants.

Scaring up Pheasants from Parked Machinery and Hiding Spots

Pheasants like to hide out in well covered areas such as brush and other areas that give them cover. In addition, they like to hide by human created hiding spots.

If you are going to be hunting on a farm you will likely run across some parked farm equipment or even some farm equipment that has been retired, never to be used again and simply left to sit in one spot forever.

These create some excellent hunting spots for you and a hunting party to shoot some pheasants. As an example, there might be an old tractor that is sitting on the side of the field collecting dust and has tall grass growing all around it. The first thing you will want to do is position a few of the hunters at surrounding locations about 20 yards away from the tractor and standing in an open area. We want these hunters to be able to see as far around the tractor as possible.

Next you will send one or two hunters to the tractor. When these hunters get to the tractor you will want them to bang with their hand or a stick on the side of the tractor, holler loud with their voice and even kick the tires of the tractor. Basically we want these people to make as much noise as possible.

Through all of the noise that these hunters are creating any pheasants that are near the tractor or hiding under the tractor are going to get scared and fly away from the area. This is exactly the scenario we want and the people who have been positioned 20 yards away from the tractor should be able to see the pheasants and get some shots at the target.

Shared Bag Limits

One benefit of party hunting for pheasants is the shared bag limits. As we discussed earlier, bag limits are the amount of birds that each individual is able to shoot in any single given day. In many areas this might be 2 or 3 rooster pheasants per day.

However, when you party hunt you are able to share these bag limits. What I mean is if you have 10 hunters and the daily bag limit is 3 birds per person then the group can shoot a cumulative total of 30 birds.

In this scenario each hunter still gets to take home 3 birds each but it allows the group to share the success. For example, if one hunter happened to be in an excellent shooting position when the group was driving out a field and they shot 10 birds alone, this means that they can share this success with the others so everyone gets to take home some pheasant meat.

Company

The final benefit of party hunting is the company that it provides. I am a person that truly enjoys hunting but the enjoyment is not all about shooting birds and animals. The majority of my enjoyment comes from spending time outdoors with my friends and family and all of the fun stories and memories that we get from each hunt.

There are not many times these days that we are able to separate from the distraction of technology and spend uninterrupted time with those who we care about. When you go hunting you are forced to make this separation from technology and simply enjoy the time with one another.

Now let's talk about hunting with the assistance of dogs…

Step 16: Hunting Pheasants with Dogs

Use the assistance of dogs to improve your success

For those who really want to increase their chances of shooting pheasants, the incorporation of dogs into your hunting strategy is a great method to choose. Pheasant hunting with dogs can be one of the most effective ways to get those pesky pheasants to come out in shooting range as they can get into spots that humans cannot.

Previously we have discussed some strategies on how to party hunt for pheasants. The power of more than one person hunting for pheasants is incredible, but if you use dogs on your trek for pheasants you may notice your success increase exponentially.

Considerations for Pheasant Hunting With Dogs:

- Where to Get Pheasant Hunting Dogs
- How a Dog Benefits the Hunt
- Safety

Where to Get Pheasant Hunting Dogs

For those hunters who are will be spending a lot of time pheasant hunting and are willing to invest in the cost of a trained dog you can consider contacting a dog kennel or training service to meet your needs.

Buying a fully trained hunting dog will usually run several hundred dollars to several thousand dollars depending on the breed of the dog and the quality of the training kennel. The nice thing about buying a fully trained dog is that you will able to get out hunting essentially right away.

Another option is you can buy a dog and bring it to a kennel to have it trained. However, dogs are most easily trainable in the first year or so of their life. If you have an older dog it will be difficult, if not impossible to have it trained into a hunting dog.

The great thing is you do not necessarily need to go out and buy a dog specifically for pheasant hunting to improve your success. If you have a dog without formal hunting experience the dog will still be likely to provide some hunting assistance. Really, all you need is a dog who will be curious enough to help sniff out the pheasants and hopefully scare a few up for you.

How a Dog Benefits the Hunt

Unlike party hunting with humans, dogs are able to get into the smallest of areas in order to flush out pheasants. Dogs have an incredible sense of smell and will be able to follow that smell to the wide range of places that pheasants will be hiding. Additionally, dogs are fast and nimble meaning that they can push pheasants to get up flying allowing you to shoot at them.

As a person hunting with a dog you get to let the dog to do the tough work for you which can make the pheasant hunting experience very relaxing. A great way to have dogs do the work for pheasant hunting is pushing out a woods or an area of thick brush.

For example, let's say there is an area of thick brush that is adjacent to an open prairie or field. You will want to send the dog into the brush and have them actively seek out pheasants. While the dog is in the brush you will be walking along side of the area that the dog is walking but you will be in the open.

When the dog happens upon a pheasant in the brush there is a good likeliness that that the dog will be able to force the pheasant to run out into the open area in front of you and start flying.

If this happens you should have some excellent shooting at the pheasant without any obstruction between you and the pheasant. You just need to give the dog the signal to "get em" and they will make their move and kick up the pheasant. After a few times of this you should be able to bag several pheasants.

Safety

The final piece that we need to discuss in regards to hunting pheasants with dogs is safety. We have already discussed safety in other sections regarding various parts of pheasant hunting. However, I want to bring it up again here because not only is hunting safety important when you are with other people, it is important when you hunt with dogs as well.

Unless you have a highly trained hunting dog, the dogs are not going to intentionally stay out of the line of fire. Please be sure that you use proper care when shooting as you want to have everyone, including your dogs, return safely from your pheasant hunting trip.

Time to discuss roadside hunting...

Step 17: Roadside Pheasant Hunting

Who Knew You Could Hunt Pheasants By The Road?

If you are a pheasant hunter who is looking or a truly heart pounding experience with your next hunt then you just might want to give roadside pheasant hunting a try.

Roadside hunting involves driving through back country roads on the look for pheasants that are on the road or in the ditches. This can be one of the most effective ways to bag a lot of birds with minimal physical effort.

Strategies for Roadside Hunting

- Laws and regulations
- Designate a driver
- Be prepared
- Move quickly

Laws and Regulations

Before you begin roadside hunting you want to be sure and check the laws and regulations for this type of hunting in your area. Some states do not allow any roadside hunting while other states allow it but in only certain areas.

You also need to check what the legal hunting area is in proximity to the road. Basically, there will be a pre-determined area that is considered the road right away that is allowed to be hunted. This is typically a certain distance from the center of the road. As an example you may be able to shoot pheasants that are within 20 yards from the center of the road.

For the most part you would use your common sense before attempting to shoot pheasants that are too far onto someone's property. A pheasant that is sitting 5 yards out in the ditch is probably ok to shoot where a pheasant that is out in the middle of a landowner's field is not going to be ok to shoot.

Designate a Driver

Depending on how many people you have hunting with you it would be a good idea to designate a person to be the driver. This person can be focused on driving safely and keeping an eye out for pheasants. Of course the passengers can help keep an eye out for pheasants as well but it will be this person's primary responsibility to get the group to pheasants.

Having a designated driver can add a level of safety to this type of experience. This way the driver will not be trying to put the vehicle in park and then quickly try to grab their gun. Rushing someone with a gun is never a good idea and could lead to the river forgetting to put the vehicle into park or an accidental discharge of the gun.

Of course this person will not get any shooting in so if you are hunting with a group of people you should share this role by having people take turns. Maybe the driver has this responsibility for 1 hour and then it gets swapped to the next person so everyone has an opportunity to shoot pheasants that day.

Be Prepared

The hunters in the vehicle will want to be prepared to get out of the vehicle as quickly as possible once the driver stops. Now in most areas you will need to have your gun cased and unloaded as you roadside hunt for pheasants. What you can do is have your gun in a spot that you can easily grab it and get it uncased.

In addition, you should have some shotgun shells in your hand or in a pocket that you can quickly grab after you get out of the vehicle and you are ready to load your shotgun.

Finally, I would recommend that you pay particular attention to your clothing when you are roadside hunting. You should be sure that your jackets are zipped and any items that could get caught on the seat of the vehicle when you exit are secure. It is never fun when you are trying to get out of a vehicle and you get caught up on the seatbelt.

Move Quickly

After you are out of the vehicle you need to get your gun loaded quickly and move fast to the pheasant. The pheasants might have noticed your vehicle pull up so if you wait too long to shoot they might take off and be gone well before you get to them.

You probably do not want to run but you can certainly walk quickly to where the pheasant is at so you could shoot them before they leave. Now if you shoot a pheasant and it then travels onto a landowner's property it is ok to retrieve that bird. Check your local regulations but as long as you shoot the bird in public space and it happens to land on private land it should be ok to retrieve. Just be sure that you do not start hunting for other birds once you cross into private property.

Now let's take a look at effective shooting techniques…

Step 18: Shooting

A Pheasant is in Sight, Now What?

When you finally have flushed out a pheasant into the open it is one of those moments that make your heart race. This moment where the pheasant is close enough to shoot will be brief so you need to quickly take action to bag the pheasant.

Use these tips to make the most out of your shooting opportunities.

Shooting Tips:

- Practice shooting before the hunting season
- Act quickly
- Select a clear shooting lane
- Shot placement
- Improving shot accuracy
- Learn from missed shots

Practice Shooting Before the Hunting Season

If you have never been pheasant hunting or if you are having difficulties hitting pheasants then it might be a good idea to get some target practice in before your next hunting trip. One of the easiest and most cost effective ways to practice shooting is to visit a gun club.

Chances are you live within ½ hour of a gun club where you can pay a fee to shoot some clay pigeons. This is usually inexpensive as you can buy a round of 25 clay pigeons for about $8-$10 and a box of target shotgun shells for around $7 for a total of less than $20. This minimal investment could greatly improve your success for your next bird outing.

This can also be a fun sport to get into during the off season. Many hunting clubs offer target shooting leagues and you could sign up with a friend and enjoy this activity a few times a month. If you did trap shooting this often there is no doubt in my mind that when the pheasant hunting season comes around you will be well prepared to shoot these challenging birds.

Act Quickly

When you are hunting pheasants you have to be ready to act quickly at any time. One second you will be walking along and maybe even letting your mind wander for just a moment and the next second a pheasant will appear and it will be making a mad dash in flight to put distance between itself and you.

In order to be able to act quickly the primary thing that you need to do is have your gun in a position where you can get it shouldered and ready to shoot fast. Do this by holding the gun with one hand on the stock, just behind the trigger area, and the other hand on the base of the barrel.

Essentially you are holding the gun with both hands in the position where you would be shooting from but instead of having the gun at your shoulder you are holding it in front of yourself while you walk.

Now it is important to think about safety as you do this. First, you always want to be sure that the gun is on the safe mode while you are walking. Second, do not have your finger inside of the trigger area until you are just ready to shoot. Trigger safeties have malfunctioned or people have thought they put their gun on safe, later to realize they didn't. Just be careful and stay away from the trigger until it is time to shoot.

Select a Clear Shooting Lane

Waiting for a clear shooting lane plays a role in both bagging pheasants as well as hunting safety. This is not always an easy task because pheasants can appear from any direction and can change direction in flight.

As you are walking you should always be scanning the area for the pheasants. While doing this you need to continually be thinking about the shooting zones that you have if a pheasant were to appear. What I mean is you need to be aware of your surroundings and anything that may be behind the area where you could be shooting.

This could include things like buildings from a farm that you are hunting on or the location of any other hunters that are in your group. Having this pre-planned out will allow you to react quickly when a pheasant does appear.

When you are party hunting in a field there will be hunters all over including some hunters in the field and some positioned at the end of the field. Make sure that the birds are plenty high in the air before you shoot.

If you are ever uncertain if you will be taking a safe shot, do not shoot! It is better to have missed an opportunity at a pheasant rather than having a chance at a terrible hunting accident.

Shot Placement

Now that a pheasant is in shooting range let's discuss where you should attempt to place your shot. If possible, the best place to hit the pheasant is in the head and chest area as an accurately placed shot here will provide a very quick and lethal kill. However, this is much easier said than done.

Anytime that you hunt birds and animals it is important to be conscious about your shot placement in order to preserve most of the meat. This is why I recommend to try and place the shot in the head and chest areas.

Now with a shotgun it is inevitable that when you shoot a pheasant there will be times where the BBs hit other parts of the body of the pheasant and that is ok. In most cases the bird will be flying away from you so you have no other choice but to shoot it from behind.

It is just that you should try to do your best to place the majority of the shot on the head so that the BBs do not end up all over on the pheasant. The thickest feathers are on the back side of the bird so when you are shooting them from behind they have the most protection from the BBs so there is a lower chance that BBs will penetrate for a kill.

Improving Shot Accuracy

One of the best ways to drastically improve your shooting accuracy is to stabilize yourself as you take a shot. This helps to keep you from swaying back and forth which will create inaccurate shots.

How do you take better shots?

- Stand with your feet planted in a parallel position to your target
- Take a deep breath just before you shot
- Lead the bird

Standing with your feet planted in a parallel position to your target is important to help improve accuracy. This position helps you line up your shot with your body so your body will be better stabilized and will allow you to handle the recoil of the first shot and prepare for a second shot if necessary.

It is surprising how difficult it is to stand still and aim effectively without being conscious of your shooting position. Essentially, to get into a good standing position for an accurate shot you want to get your feet planted parallel to where you are shooting.

Think of this as taking one arm and pointing directly out to the side of your body and that will be the location where you will have the most shooting accuracy. When you are ready to aim simply align your shoulders to the direction that you are going to shoot and raise up your gun.

You should also pay attention to your breathing as you get ready to shoot. To stabilize your shot you want to take a deep breath just before you shoot. Breathing causes the gun to move up and down. As you get into shooting position and are just about ready to take your shot take a deep breath. Then aim and slowly let your breath out. You should find that this technique greatly improves the accuracy of your shots.

Finally, you should pay attention to leading your bird with your shots. What leading means is aiming for a spot that is slightly ahead of where the pheasant currently is. Pheasants typically get up and head straight in the direction they are flying, they are not known for making fast adjustments with the flight direction they are heading.

Let's say you are a hunter who is party hunting and you are one of the hunters who are positioned at the end of the field where the walking hunters are trying to push pheasants to. When you see a pheasant heading your way you should get your gun up and in a shooting position and wait for the bird to get close.

When it is getting close imagine a spot just a few inches in front of the bird as it heads your direction. Once the bird hits that spot go ahead and pull the trigger. This slight leading of the bird will cause the BBs to hit the bird because it takes just a moment for you to pull the trigger and for the BBs to travel to the bird. By doing this the BBs should make good contact with the bird and provide a good kill shot.

Learn From Missed Shots

Any pheasant hunter regardless if they are experienced or novice has missed shots at pheasants. I tell you this because it is important to not let yourself get down when you miss. Pheasants are very fast and often are running through thick underbrush or flying away quickly.

Use missed shots as an opportunity to learn from your mistakes. Try and evaluate what you did well and what you could have done differently. Did you get into a stable shooting position for an accurate shot? Did you allow the pheasant to get into a clear opening? Did you shoot too soon?

These are all questions to ask yourself in order to improve upon your shooting success. After more time hunting your hit rates will improve but keep in mind that it is tough to have 100% accuracy and that is completely ok and normal.

Keep reading to learn how to retrieve the pheasant you just shot...

Step 19: Retrieving Your Pheasant

You Hit the Pheasant, Now What?

After you shoot a pheasant you will want to retrieve your game. Use these tips to be the most effective after shooting at a pheasant...

Tips after Shooting:

- Memorize where you shot at the pheasant
- Walk slowly to the pheasant
- Check to ensure the pheasant is dead before you grab it

Memorize Where you Shot at the Pheasant

If you shoot a pheasant it will often fall from the spot they were and drop dead immediately. This means that for the majority of the time it should not be difficult to find the pheasant that you shot. However, I encourage you to not let your mind get too excited from you're your hunting success until you locate your pheasant.

The reason I want to encourage you to keep mentally aware after you shoot the pheasant is that when you are hunting in a field or area that has a lot of brush, the areas can all blend together. Even walking 30 yards can seem to change the look of the area and make it difficult to locate your pheasant. So what you want to do is as soon as you shoot you should look for any other markings in the field or brush that are by where the pheasant was shot.

For example, pick out a tall or darker colored corn stock in the area that you can use as a location marker to walk to. Depending on the area you are hunting the corn and brush can cover up the pheasant and make it difficult to find unless you have a way remember the exact spot it fell.

Walk Slowly to the Pheasant

While you walk to the spot the pheasant you shot, it is important to proceed slowly. Sometimes you may have just wounded the pheasant so you want to keep an eye on the ground and brush to look for any movement. On the off chance the pheasant is alive and moving across the ground it may be necessary to shoot it again.

The other reason you want to walk slowly to the pheasant is to look for any other pheasants in the immediate area. It is not uncommon for more than one pheasant to be in the same area so even through you shot one pheasant there may still be another one hiding that you might kick up as you attempt to retrieve your first pheasant. Bagging two pheasants at one time is very satisfying.

Check to Ensure the Pheasant is Dead Before you Grab it

Before you pick up the pheasant it is very important to ensure that the pheasant is dead. I am giving you this warning because if you pick up a pheasant that is still alive the chances are you will get scratched. In most cases, particularly if you shot the pheasant in the head, it will be dead immediately. However, do not take any chances and do a quick test just to be sure.

An easy way to do this is by grabbing a stick that is on the ground and poke the pheasant to see if it moves. The majority of the time they will be dead but if they show any movement at all you need to quickly finish off the pheasant.

Step on the pheasant's body with your boots to pin the pheasant down and then take out your hunting knife and cut the throat and neck area of the pheasant. This is never a fun task but it is important to be humane and get the pheasant out of any suffering as soon as possible.

Keep reading to learn how to clean the pheasant you just shot...

Step 20: Pheasant Cleaning

Success! You Shot a Pheasant, Now What?

Once you bagged your pheasant it is time to clean it. It is important to prepare your pheasant to take home soon after shooting it. This is because the internal organs of the pheasant can actually cause the meat to spoil.

This is even more important if it is warm out. In cold temperatures the pheasant can sit a little longer but on a warm day you should try and clean it immediately.

You do not need to clean the pheasant the instant that you shoot it because you might not be done with hunting yet and you might shoot a few more pheasants that you need to clean. However, it would be good to clean the pheasants within two hours of shooting it.

Note: This will get messy. Some people purchase disposable plastic cleaning gloves to try and stay as clean as possible.

Steps to Clean Your Pheasant:

STEP 1: Lay the pheasant on its back on the ground. Using our hands take one wing of the bird and pull it into an open/expanded position as if the bird had its wings fully spread.

STEP 2: Step on the wing close to the side of the chest of the bird. Do this so the wing stays fully open with the inside of your foot touching the side of the chest of the bird. Also be sure to have as much of the bottom of your foot on top of the wing so that it is tightly pinned to the ground.

STEP 3: Repeat this process with the other wing and step on the 2nd wing with your other foot so you are standing over the bird with both of the wings spread wide open.

STEP 4: Now grab the pheasant's legs. Use one hand per leg. Pull up towards yourself with the legs at a slight angle away from your head. You will need to pull pretty hard but you will soon notice the bird begin to separate. Keep pulling until you have completely separated the legs and bottom section of the bird from the chest and wings.

STEP 5: You will now have cleanly exposed chest section of the pheasant left behind on the ground with the wings attached. Take a meat scissors and cut off the wings of the pheasant at the joints so all you have left behind is the chest cavity.

STEP 6: Use a knife to cut the breast meat away from the chest bone. Do this by cutting down the middle of the chest plate and slowly working your knife along the breast plate on one side of the bird. Once you have removed one breast, repeat to remove the second breast.

STEP 7: Now that you have both breasts removed you will want to rinse off any feathers from the breasts with water and trim off any excess fat that may be left behind. It is also important to examine the meat for any BBs. Look for puncture holes and feel inside of them to pull out the BBs.

Now it's time to enjoy your pheasant…

Step 21: Time to Enjoy Your Pheasant!

Preparing a simple yet delicious pheasant dish

A great thing about the sport of pheasant hunting is that it provides joy and excitement while you are out hunting but it also provides an incredible meal when you are done with your hunting trip.

I find it very satisfying to share the game I shot with friends and family. The flavor of pheasant is unique it is a great conversation piece when as you sit around the dinner table.

The good news is that you can cook pheasant you shot in a very simple way that turns out incredibly good. Preparation time for the meal is just a few minutes and the ingredients are minimal and common around the house.

How to Fry Pheasant

Ingredients:

- 4 fresh shot pheasant breasts
- Flour
- Seasoned salt
- Canola oil
- Frying pan with high edges
- Large Tupperware style storage container
- Kitchen tongs
- Paper towels

STEP 1: Add 1 cup of flour and 4 tablespoons of seasoned salt to the inside of your Tupperware style storage container.

STEP 2: Close the lid and shake up the flour and salt until the two ingredients mixed together well.

STEP 3: Open up the storage container and place the pheasant pieces into the storage container. Close the lid and shake the pheasant up in the container for about 10-15 seconds until the pieces are covered on all sides with the flour and salt mixture.

STEP 4: Place your frying pan on the stove and pour enough canola oil in the pan so you have about 1 inch of oil on the bottom of the pan. Turn the heat to medium-high and allow preheating for approximately 5 minutes.

STEP 5: Take the pheasant pieces and place them in the hot oil. You will want to use kitchen tongs to grab the meat off the Tupperware and gently place the meat into the oil. As you place the meat in the oil let the bottom of the piece touch the pan first and then gently place the rest of the meat down in a direction away from you. By placing the meat down away from you it will help keep the hot oil from splashing back onto you.

STEP 6: Let the meat cook for 2-3 minutes on the first side and then flip the meat over using your kitchen tongs. You will know when the meat is ready when the first side is golden brown.

STEP 7: After both sides of the pheasant have been cooked to a golden brown color place the pheasant pieces on a plate that is covered with about 2-3 paper towels. Having the paper towels on the plate will help soak up the excess oil.

STEP 8: Sprinkle a little of the seasoned salt on both sides of the meat to your personal level of taste.

STEP 9: Allow the pheasant to cool for about 5 minutes and then enjoy the meal that you shot.

Bonus #1 Accelerate Your Pheasant Hunting Success

Shorten Your Learning Curve at a Game Farm
Visiting a pheasant game farm for one day is a great way to dramatically speed up learning how to be successful with hunting pheasants.

Guides at pheasant game farms have expert knowledge of hunting techniques and even one guided trip can help you greatly.

What can you learn from a guide at game farm?

- Hunting strategies
- Shooting techniques
- Bird identification
- Locations
- Bird cleaning

How do I Find a Pheasant Game Farm?

If you do a Google search for "pheasant game farms' in whatever area you are looking to hunt you will likely find several location. Another place that you may find pheasant game farms advertised is Craigslist.

Where to Find Game Farms:

- Internet search
- Craigslist
- Guide booking agents
- Outdoor expos

What will it Cost to go to a Game Farm?

Although there are a variety of ways that a pheasant game farm could charge its clients, the most common type of fee structure is the per bird released structure. Basically, you pay for a certain amount of birds that the game farm will release into the fields that you will be hunting.

The game farm will send someone out with those birds a few hours before you go hunting so you hopefully get a chance at shooting them. Of course the more birds you buy the better the chances are that you will see and shoot birds. Most game farms have a minimum amount of birds that you must purchase. Often you will get lucky and there will be some birds that are left from the previous hunting parties that you can shoot at as well.

Average rates:

- $15-$30 per bird released
- $2-$5 per bird for cleaning
- $3-$6 per bird to have a guide with dog

Factors that typically impact the cost:

- Time of season, usually there are premium rates for popular weekends
- Amount of birds you want released
- Number of people that will be hunting
- Bird cleaning fees

Final Words as You Start Pheasant Hunting

Congratulations! You have taken your first step in becoming a successful pheasant hunter.

Your Success is in Your Hands

If you have made it this far it is clear that you are passionate about pheasant hunting and you want to shoot more pheasants. Remember that hunting is fun but also challenging. Regardless of the success you have ensure you take time to enjoy the time you spend outdoors.

Just Get Started

Getting started with anything can be challenging at first. Think back to when you first started tying your shoes. At first it was difficult but after time it became second nature. This can be the same with pheasant hunting. The more you do it the better you will get.

Make Progress Every Day

Using the steps learned in this book will help improve your pheasant hunting skills. I encourage you to make some type of progress each day of the season. Keep reading books, follow hunting blogs and watch YouTube videos. Six months from now you will be surprised how far you have made it by spending time learning more about pheasant hunting each day.

Want to Learn More About Hunting?

Check out my other books on Amazon:

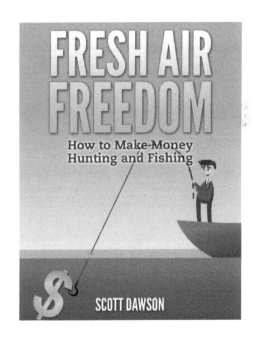

Finally, please take 1 minute to leave a review.

I truly hope that the information in this book was useful to you and that I have earned a 5 star review. Reviews help others find this book and allows people to see how the information can help them. It also allows me to keep writing useful books like this for you to enjoy in the future. Visit my author page to leave your review: http://bit.ly/scottsauthorpage

 I love it

Reviews help because:

- It helps me write more books that you can enjoy in the future

- It helps other people find this book

- It helps others know how this information can help them

- It is encouraging to hear how my books have helped others enjoy the outdoors

Thank you and good luck hunting!

Sincerely,

Scott Dawson

Your Free Gift

As a way of saying thank you for your purchase, I'm offering a copy of my book that is extremely useful for people who are passionate about hunting.

In *"21 Simple Steps to Save Big Money on Hunting Equipment",* you will learn my stratigies to help you save 30% or more on hunting gear. My goal is to help people get into hunting regardless of their budget.

Visit http://bit.ly/savemoneyonhunting to Grab Your FREE Copy of "21 Simple Steps to Save Big Money on Hunting Equipment".

Made in the USA
Columbia, SC
08 May 2018